Daughter

Patricia Helen Wooldridge

LEAF BY LEAF

Published by Leaf by Leaf
an imprint of Cinnamon Press
www.cinnamonpress.com

The right of Patricia Helen Wooldridge to be identified as author of this work has been asserted by her in accordance with the Copyright, Designs and Patent Act, 1988. © 2022, Patricia Helen Wooldridge.
ISBN 978-1-78864-944-5

British Library Cataloguing in Publication Data. A CIP record for this book can be obtained from the British Library. All rights reserved. No part of this publication may be reproduced, stored in a retrieval system, or transmitted in any form or by any means, electronic, mechanical, photocopying, recording or otherwise without the prior written permission of the publishers. This book may not be lent, hired out, resold or otherwise disposed of by way of trade in any form of binding or cover other than that in which it is published, without the prior consent of the publishers.

Designed and typeset in Bodoni by Cinnamon Press.
Cover design by Adam Craig © Adam Craig.
Cinnamon Press is represented by Inpress

Acknowledgements

I wish to thank the editors of the following publications where some of these poems have appeared occasionally in slightly different versions: 'For the Love of Madonna Lilies, 1938' appeared in *Envoi 181* February 2019 and 'Death's Architecture' appeared in *Envoi 184* April 2020. 'Knit Forward, Purl Back' was published in the anthology *Journey Planner*, ed. Rowan B. Fortune, Cinnamon Press, 2014. 'Walking with Edward Thomas' was published in the anthology *From Hallows to Harvest* ed. Adam Craig, Cinnamon Press, 2019. 'Black Windows' and 'I plant tulips, winter beans…' were both published in *Agenda* (supplement), December 2020. 'You Nearly Called Me Sylvia' was published in *Artemispoetry* May 2021.

I would like to thank Jan Fortune at Cinnamon Press for all the help and advice given during the 2019 mentorship scheme while working on the earlier stages of this collection.

My thanks also go to my fellow poets from our Sussex 'post doctoral' poetry group for all their support and helpful advice.

I would like to give special thanks to Ann Williams who gave such warm support and thoughtful comments in the final reading of this collection.

Finally I would like to say thank you to my husband for all his interest, encouragement and generous willingness to listen to my thoughts over the years whilst writing these poems.

for my mother and father

Contents

Preludes

In Black and White	10
Leaving the Mirror	11
With the Michaelmas Daisies	12
Long Division	13
The Index of Laughter	14
Black Windows	15
Stone Head	16
Your Tiny Hand is Frozen	17
The End of the Line	18
Knit Forward, Purl Back	19
You Nearly Called Me Sylvia	20

Variations

Anderson Shelter, 1940	22
Blackout	23
Fog	24
God's Pocket	25
Exploding Matter	26
Lathe	27
Ilfracombe	28
Jettison	29
K is for…	30
Morecambe, 1942	31
V2 on New Year's Day	32
Your oak table…	33
Home	34
Unsaid	35
Sister	36
Wedding Photograph	37
Portraits	38
Rosebay Willow-herb	39
Questions	40
Night Walk	41
Over	42
Death's Architecture	44
At the Crematorium	46
X, Y, Z	47

Fugue

Lacuna	50
Lacuna	51
Yet all things follow from the word	52
Loss	53
I plant tulips, winter beans...	54
Walking with Edward Thomas	56
I loved your crystal vase...	57
Little things...	58
The sun's shrinking hole...	59
The Right Kind of Snow	60
For the Love of Madonna Lilies, 1938	61

Daughter

*for the present when backed by the past
is a thousand times deeper than the present...*

Virginia Woolf, *A Sketch of the Past*

Preludes

walk among magnolias
where the sun raises lily-rose
straight from the cup

like an answer from a tree of egrets

In Black and White

The blackbird startles from the homestead hedge
                                           John Clare

In the beginning it is always September,
buzzards calling, a week of warm weather,
forecast balmy, early drizzle as I write
in the blackbird's silence, linger in the light,

picking, like my garden birds, yielding to words,
ripe as elderberries rolling in my hand,
purple milk in my mouth, this late summer end.

With pencil and paper and looming clouds,
a blink of sun-dog heralds this smattering of rain,
the tractor drones, tilling methodical stripes,
scattered harebells, hawk-bit, patches of eyebright,

a post-war baby, lying on a hill, trying to explain –
while buzzards ride these upward draughts,
I know these poems are not still photographs.

Leaving the Mirror

By the open window that hasn't closed
all week, I'm sure I watched some people
standing in my view – they waved and climbed
the hill – were they ever there?

Wearing my mother's scarf, I leave my folded
nightwear, faintly warm, underneath the pillow.
The weather will be rain, sun and a long-shore
drift, gulls a flicker of white handkerchiefs.

How is the sea today? Foamy; fans spuming
over my boots and the wind is rousing
a see-saw flail. I am the woman sliding down
these banks of stone without an easy way up.

All along the strand line, beaks to the wind,
gulls are nestling voices...

With the Michaelmas Daisies

When it's this quiet with the Michaelmas daisies
promising mauve, bedding in with the fuchsia cutting

I took from yours – the best it's been – I think of you,
a woman of twenty-two I never knew.

Married more than a year, hope is possible
with your new son; you may live in only two rooms

with a landlord forbidding nappies on the line,
but it's Richmond Hill, a stone's throw from the cliff

looking down on the river, a walk over common
land, to reach Ham and your mother.

Today the swathes of long cut grass, a heron leaning,
frayed moon in opposing blush of sunrise –

none of us know how we look with the loss of self
in laying out, how they never return your floral nightdress.

Long Division

and a nightingale sang in Berkeley Square

Stepping out on the first morning of frost,
like walking on crepe paper, leaves drip
and fall, a wave of colour flooding.

The morning gave you chores, keep things
tidy, mop the kitchen floor, walk to shops –

for you walk everywhere, use the bus or train,
never owned a car. You might have put out
the washing, swept the path, and I may make

eighty-four years, like you and your mother.
That's nine hundred and thirty six Sundays
(remaining) or, a jar full of marbles.

Through the curling eye of this Sunday,
I hear the woodlark singing in October,
lucid, fluent, as any nightingale.

The Index of Laughter

The trees are vaporous in their hoar.
Another Christmas with us before: *I feel weak
as a kitten*. The rime clings, overlays this black
and white – who am I like?

How odd it was to see them with friends,
singing round the piano – the old songs –
his arm resting on her, smiling like their wedding
photograph, roses painted in red.

The time we joined her in the hospital room –
it was her husband who had died. She in the calm
after worry over, telling us to get a cup of tea.
Dad had been the one to joke: *when you're dead, you're dead.*

Ordering the double-sided memorial plaque, she knew
he would have said: *two for the price of one* as I did.

Black Windows

Fifty-five coots, vocal ducks and miserable swans
over this moon-lake,

ice debris and twisted logs aping the death of birds;
one moorhen clings to the reeds

in minus nine and the fog has bristled this coldest
December since yours of 47 –

the Thames in partial freeze, a sun rubbed out.

How you would have shivered in your basement flat,
black windows with a frozen crust –

but I'm glad I came this way when the egret
floats through the alders,

lands on the island and preens. Such a grubby white
it seems against this snow,

rose-grey between the trees – the spectral lift.

Stone Head

        That hint of old ponds
as it starts to rain, reflections muddied and a year
        ceases to mean anything,

the smell of farmland, damp wool,
        where the sheep-bitten hill slips
from the soak of winter, rippling down –

to where one stone head wears a wrap around shawl…

it could be Gran in our garden, living on threadbare days,
        ten children and Dad one of nine survived –
he has the same thin-lipped smile,

overhead sun shivering silver on the apple tree
        he planted and a bubble
of his daughter's voice
        swells beside the chestnut fencing.

Your Tiny Hand is Frozen

He would be still, in his chair, the music
combing his bones like mine now.
And when my cat had to be put down,
he cried (Mum told me later).

Pushing the mower, forward and back,
it takes time – sharpen blades –
the smell of cut grass, Dad burning
leaves, Mum in brown slacks pruning,

keeps him from brooding – look how the sun
shimmers blue-green on a magpie's back –
forget when he comes in the kitchen,
picks up the teapot to put on the gas.

Once, I saw them as they sat together
on the settee, holding hands, listening.

The End of the Line

> *For we think back through our mothers if we are women*
> Virginia Woolf, *A Room of One's Own*

In the walking glow of a March morning, the light
dazzling, a neighbour's washing swinging
into view – it's a generation thing – no rotaries here

but looped, fence to fence, prop ready to lift
big white pants, vests, shirts, like my mother's
line, only we had a concrete post, honeysuckled

with a blackbird's nest. Watching, I wonder
will the fence hold in this sailing wind? Monday's
routine, pegging out the week's linen, a toil that

hasn't changed much from laying on a bush to dry,
or slack lines between tenement windows
as if everything could be sorted and achieved

by hanging out the washing on a fine day in spring.

Knit Forward, Purl Back

A life of all our jumpers, baby clothes, Dad's cardigans
to four rows at the day centre, a bag with your name on,
telling me how the ladies revolt, refuse and stop –

all we do is sit and knit, we don't know why or who for –
one casts hers off and says it'll do as a floor cloth.
Doing your rows at the back – it passes the time until lunch.

The stocking stitch chat of needles, the stroke of wool
winding through your fingers, catching up on the tick
of the clock at home, the rhythm of unshared thinking,

broken in a glance – a painted bird you've never seen,
hopping on the lawn. Reaching for the phone, you ask me:
such a pink-brown, black and white with a checked splash of blue,

huge beside the sparrow.

A jay in your garden, alarm caller through the bluebell woods
where I picked drooping stems an acorn flight from our door.

You Nearly Called Me Sylvia

What was I looking for scrabbling about in
the shallow stream? Rushing down after rain,

overspill filling the woods with deluge,
rising high into our road, boats on the street,

no way through for weeks – round the long way
to ballet, point and dance, hold the arabesque,

fingers for grace, as if my life could be
etched by bluebells in their hanging crooks –

each glade a flickering world of rivulets
to scramble into – pre-sunrise,

a pair of barn owls glide on silence,
lose themselves into hollows,

a red-ball-sun slots into cloud –
walk on, deep in the woods, the depth of *what if...*

Variations

the dark sleeks over the wall
curls up next to me —
my eye on the thin moon

Anderson Shelter, 1940

It was their side of the road not ours. *

Cold daylight.

The garden wet with dewy cobwebs
and you're still shaking from the blast.

Your mother (limping in her Parkinson's gait)
opens the back door to a shower of white,

shakes the kettle and says: *let's have some tea,*
with that half-smile she had on greeting.

Your sister Kathy clears the table with a dust pan
and brush, Peggy picks up the unbroken cups...

You never mention the taste of burning
in the morning after, how you pee in a bucket,

six of you huddling for warmth all night
with a candle and flask of tea.

Only how you venture round the front to find
your aunt's house sliced open, stairs going nowhere,

a direct hit on their garden shelter...

And cousin Margaret (who'd refused to go in there)
floating like an angel in her white night-dress.

* *the words of my mother*

Blackout

rim of the earth in embers
orange ball flares
does infinity exist?

You never liked the dark. So dark your eyes
seemed to melt into black, night after night.

That first winter, coming home on the bus –
barely enough glow to get off at the stop,

holding on to the hedge, feeling your way,
a blind woman, counting steps to each turn.

A full moon was worse – there would be raids –
the Thames leading the way...

Now it's hard to find jelly-black pricking with stardust.
The street lights blaze, even on a hill out of town,

nothing but pulsing, orange beacons.

But walking down a country lane I can't find my footing –
feel I'm falling, see nothing and sweat fear.

Fog

Still the fog hangs...

even so, great tits ringing,
starlings deep probe
on the lawn and

a baby won't stop crying –
why doesn't she pick it up?

I wish I could remember mother comforting.

Still the fog hangs...

Mum and Dad trying to get home
in the raid –

you can't see your hands,
inching your way,
the Thames slaps so close –

you stumble against the quayside post...

God's Pocket

when I draw round my hands
a live line shivers
like an ancient footprint

Stale bread in the brown paper bag softens in my hand.
Breaking the crust from Nan's *Hovis* loaf – throwing it

to the back of the pond where the less greedy wait –
the sucking, bubbling, beaks. Or Mum and her sisters,

running from the house in a minute to feed the ducks,
then round the corner to the hidden church behind trees,

sitting on the step outside listening to their one brother
singing, before the war.

Visiting a mock air raid shelter, they play muffled bombs,
leak a puff of smoke, shake the walls – nothing like at all.

I hear someone say *we're in God's pocket*
and I'm glad she never said that.

Here by the water with its willow-frilled edge, an umbrella
and spaniel going past, everything soaked, I have a line,

it floats like gossamer, I don't write it down –
it blows clean away.

Exploding Matter

after Cornelia Parker, *Cold Dark Matter: An Exploded View*

I always bring you *Old Spice* at Christmas
picture you in your whites –
a skinny dad with snowball hair

the two of us staying up all night
watching first steps on the moon

a union man with principles
who hugged me close on leaving

upstairs the full set
of blue encyclopaedias –

the black hole reels you in…

a fragment of response and smile
collapsing to a denser form of now –

your shaving soap
a cricket bat
brush and comb

coming downstairs
ask Mum
when are we going home?

Lathe

Dad – skilled turner in reserved occupation
shows the women how to operate the lathe.

Deafening, non-stop, twelve hour shifts
beside a handful of men kept from the war.

Never mind the overalls, the headscarf tied
round curled dark hair, he sees beyond this.

Mum – hates the clanging from next-door's
beaters in the body shop building trucks,

stands at the capstan-lathe: chuck, stop, drill,
metal filings worm into shoes, into underwear,

tang of iron swills in coolant, oil sweats
on the floor – his world, precision engineering.

Thrum of machines serenade first meeting.

Ilfracombe

Swim, looking out to sea, summer of 44,
away from incendiary bombs and nights on fire-watch,
the droning planes cruising up the Thames.

Never been but everyone says the place to go –
a one-week honeymoon begins with a bus ride
passing by gaping buildings, rubble and weeds.

Paddington, boarding the train with two small cases
to Devon-by-sea. That glistening view, guest-house
painted white and blue, a couple breathing in June,

finding sand in your shoes – maybe test bare feet
in the water for I know you can swim
since eleven years old but Dad never could.

I imagine you, a slim twenty-one in new costume,
modesty panels, greeting wave after wave.

Jettison

sleep the lost hour back
meet cold stars
frost-flower reverie

And here in the woods, one after another,
craters so deep it would have taken
a double-decker bus like she said,

seventy years of tree growth filling in the
jettisoned load this hazy October, high
on the downs. For Mum, the after-throws:

rubble homes, minced glass, a bus keeled
front first in the hole along the street,
rags of clothing ripped from drawers,

one bristle brush with hair still tangled
on a dresser of stones, crockery strewn,
a cup with tea-leaves…

K is for...

the killing of thousands
but the one death
Mum recounts to me
is the little black kitten
she found drowned
in the water-tank
kept in the street
to put out the fires

Morecambe, 1942

while gulls stretch
their hand-drawn wings
on paper sky...

that constant wind against your face, damp frizzling rain,
you with another hundred women, far away from home.

Each overcast day reaffirms that hole in your stomach,
tiny but slowly nibbling out your insides.

You won't know how blue this sea can shimmer, when
flames of phosphorescence are a living silver skin.

In the threads of a dying summer, increasing winds,
a salt wall of air coursing through your clothes –

photographs, talks, marching on the promenade
beside open sands too treacherous to walk on.

Standing up straight in your five feet three inches,
polished brogue leather shoes, you chose the WAAFs

because, like so many, you liked the shade of airforce blue.
Feet tucked together, black stockings, knee length skirt

blown against your legs, belt pulled close –
I begin to see the mother I knew...

sinking into sand
ground from the sea
shadows crouch behind

V2 on New Year's Day

And they came without warning – no point now
in sirens or blackouts, not a chance of running
like you did from the doodlebug...

> *a V2 the wrong way up, two floors high –*
> *this polished floor of museum busyness*
> *clustering round the hanging bomb...*

when the engine cut, scooting underneath
the archway bridge. That savage winter
and first married of 44...

> *the blurb listing feats of German engineering,*
> *with a note on prisoners of war hidden*
> *in bunkers, slaving to build these missiles...*

things to worry about – keep the fire in,
find food and enough wool to knit
your matinee coat, make it through to spring.

Your oak table...

you keep a runner on
to hide the stain
they didn't show you,

bought second-hand in the war.

I write half a page, age seven,
red book, thin lines,
wanting to tell something –

in the corner, a *Singer*
encased in oak,
full of cotton reels –

something about bobbins
locking together
yours and mine –

gift to charity,
then finding the receipt –
you were only eighteen.

Sitting at the table,
in my house now,
garden puddled in snow,

I hunger for the right words.

Home

Dad, alone at a table for tea,
crying because we are leaving

without him —
I want to go home...

round and round the corridor
at night, searching for Mum —

pool of urine under his chair,
(look at his eyes)

I want to go home...

a sitting room the size of our kitchen
packed with ten chairs,

no-one on duty —
trying to find him somewhere better...

after the third fall —
hospital, rehydration,

don't touch me
yelled in the ward —

we're asked to wait outside...

feeding him dribbles of ice cream —
a nurse says:

at least you can hold his hand.

Unsaid

Waving me off, going back inside alone,
locking the door, sleep maybe...

Better to have died of the first stroke.

Rise, make tea, keep to routine –
television, newspaper, tablets, post...

Should have died in her first collapse
stage four ovarian cancer...

Wait for me to come – hoover, do shopping,
pay bills, check everything is done.

Did she gain anything from four more
years in widowhood?

Hospital appointments, another routine
– the oncologist looking at me –

let's see how it goes...

Sister

living in a doll's house
knit a jumper for my doll
the one with short bobbed hair

Someone chose to catch this second daughter, age seven
(written on the back), standing outside a large white door.

As her doll nestles against her left arm she squints at the sun,
a shadow pooled behind in mothering.

Something familiar in the cropped style, top-knot ribbon
and baby-sized doll with the frizzy hair.

I regard her scuffed leather shoes with a one-strap buckle,
grey socks loose at the ankles, cotton frock tied at the hip.

At your wedding she cradles her baby; the next,
she's holding her hand (Joanie tottering).

You tell me she lost her to scarlet fever not long after.
Your sister, the spitting image of you

dies from cancer age fifty-eight.
I trace something round her mouth, see that ribbon

you placed in my short cropped hair.
You die the same day years later.

Wedding Photograph

Was it always on the dresser in their bedroom?
She would come and do her hair at the dressing table,
put clothes away, leave the bed made –

didn't want carers coming into their space

never spoke about him,
but little bowls of resentment spilled:

*wanted to go away for weekends,
like her friend Doris on bargain breaks to Eastbourne*

*never liked all those union meetings,
or me helping to deliver his 'Tribune' papers*

talking to his work-mates in the street,
one she never wanted to see,
bristled if she saw him walking up the road –

*she had to get Dad away from him talking loud
and brash with working-class written on his sleeves*

white taffeta embroidered with silver,
a halo head-dress of orange blossom,
rose bouquet and trailing fern…

it was me who suggested putting it downstairs
where she now spent her time,
put it downstairs where it didn't belong.

Portraits

My father in a Lowry painting,
    a man with his cap among many,
Friday sweets in his inside pocket,
    strides home from his shift,
stoops on the mat to take off shoes –
    I run to meet him

September fog smoking out the sun
dried umbellifers drooling webs…

my mother in her pink housecoat
    dusting, when the future of
post-war Britain wears sensible shoes,
    carries a fold-up umbrella
and a handbag I remember
    in black patent leather

rough field lifts its shimmering sheet
in a trickle of breeze…

a summer's day on Cooden Beach,
    railway line, halt, step to shore,
Mum and Dad on towels, fish-paste
    sandwiches, my feet wading
through knee-high greasy ropes
    trying to find the sea –

when the green-grey drowns the ribbed
sand centuries ago…

Rosebay Willow-herb

for your daughter

Flowers in June,
full bloom on her birthday,

dark pink spires,
full of bees

stunning en masse,
colonising bomb sites...

you knit her first matinee coat
in three-ply pink

layer in tissue
for your bottom drawer,

see her toddling
over cropped grass,

take a rug and picnic
to the common,

fairy cakes
wrapped in greaseproof...

stare across the river Thames –
so many unexploded bombs

the doodlebug whine
still in your head,

the weeds are growing –
blazing pink of rosebay willow-herb,

fruiting capsules
with long white plumes

carried in such numbers
the air is full of flying seeds,

growing best on dry ground,
strongest after fire.

Questions

What is your favourite colour?

> Red.

> (The red rug you make
> for the fireplace

> lasts the life-time in our house,
> each strand knotted into canvas

> at the dining room table).

What is your favourite flower?

> Rose.

> (For all the climbers
> on the arch in the garden,

> the hybrid teas lining the front path,
> the *Whisky Mac* Dad prunes too hard).

What do you most wish for?

> A daughter –

> (who wears a red cotton dress
> cut on the circle

> spinning round and round
> in a garden growing red roses

> pink rose-buds
> on her bedroom wall).

Why is there no picture of you
    holding me as a baby?

Night Walk

The thought beneath so slight a film
                                Emily Dickinson

He strolls along my head path.
I discover his gait as a young man

striding out from the station –
tall, weighty, coded in my bones,

passed down to stop here.
And I'm struck how the dead need clothes.

Mum and I choose a respectable
suit and shirt, but what about the tie?

Mum is better after seeing him dressed,
going in on her own, glad.

I read Emily Dickinson
alone with Dad. I do not speak of this.

Over

*this morning the smell of wet dog
over the mown field – a kestrel
working the same tree line...*

 in the slow outdoors, Dad's
 bowling arm, full whites –

 my brother in his romper suit,
 bare feet in the grass

 here between the two of you –

 I take a picture of my shadow
 searching for dust motes –

*stepping through the mizzled growth –
the smell of disused summer,
jackdaws munching on ash seeds...*

 Barnes unexpectedly green,
 his old school – Edwardian,

 the heath still common land
 under a Heathrow flight path –

 low jets, wheels down,
 deafening every minute –

*the surge of autumn winds
bedding in winter saturation,
a recital for voice...*

 alone on his cricket pitch Dad
 looks into bright sun

 new town calling...

 an almost smile and his thick
 crimped hair he never lost –

how Mum marks in her
People's Friend diary

next to the date: *Syd died.*

Death's Architecture

The hospice nurse takes a stem
from the vase on the window sill,
sets the red carnation beside your head...

    one whole day I come and go,
    before they bear you away
    in a black zip-up bag

    while the undertaker keeps us talking
    in the living room and I do not hear
    them close the door...

here at the funeral home,
the red carnation in your overlapped hands –
I had not put it there.

    *

A woman in one piece
holds on to the edge...

    mother and daughter
    welling across the glass

by the undrawn window a table
under the weight of an unlit room.

    *

A raven over the allotment,
gather up leeks, carrots, sprouts,
walk home laden.

    Pick up my pen...
    clouds broken, northerly,
    much the same as then,

    candles lit to see out the light,
    your smiling face –
    look how the snowdrops sprinkle the lawn...

they survive their move,
honesty coins caught in the in-between –
that's when you stopped breathing.

At the Crematorium

Do Not Stand at my Grave and Weep

Beside the powdered ash
in the same spot as Dad

    crows in open beak
    horizontal cawing

how could they know
when they lay a blood-red rose

    clouds in rags
    from the north

this was your marriage flower?

X, Y, Z

seven kisses on every card he ever gave you

from your loving sweetheart xxxxxx

from your ever-loving husband to be xxxxxx

from your ever-loving husband xxxxxx

of sixty years

I arrange a telegram from the Queen

the two of you hanging by a thread

on your diamond wedding

X-ray visions

to guide me through the lens

of seven kisses on every card

kept in paper bags too raw to lose

persistent rain

enough to make the windows cry

every night the Zeitgeist

spilling out on cobwebs to dry

Fugue

sun on a frosted field
like a voice that spills
jewels in the grass

Lacuna

tissue and veins   spreading into wings
the kind of blue mother liked to wear
going out in her coat

tiny egg under a leaf,
hatch and rasp   curlicues in green

satiate   cocoon
to hang in some dark corner

a chrysalis   to eat away
what has to be done   give me
mother in her garden   hydrangea blue

Where am I in a pile of words before snowlight seeps in?

living on the landing...

even if I stop (the clock) take away its hands
there is still the reach of hours and hours

it doesn't matter what the time is...

I could stand by (storm clouds) ignore this (face)
but when the tide is out how long before (the flood)

I will be long gone (into rock-face)

empty   chair   a soul perched
on its back   will not stay
in this windowscape   a poem unvoiced

*

Lacuna

Somewhere the sea is heaving...

wash sky with my mother's silk slip
cover the sea with her blue blouse

as if grieving could disperse in shingle

where the mouth speaks in whispers
and doesn't scream

What is sun but a ball of fire heating into mist?

a pheasant's red eye breaking cover
skimming over edge

reaching...

exhalation in the tunnel of trees –
light-fire-streams to lily-pad the road

Pencil   greys   pinned paper
I hush into   light and shade
floating in a calm sea   out of depth

but oh that weight of walking from water...

Yet all things follow from the word
Heraclitus

There is a folded place where the word
flakes into quiet

the ebb-time, pen-down time, strolling back
in gathering dark

a tawny owl scrambles up from the dead tree,
lifts onto sugared-almond sky...

I have laid out my stones – here on the table
in the room where mother died,

my father in a corridor looking back –
her loss made her speechless

she *ought to sort Dad's clothes* –
my husband wears my father's winter coat

out in the snow... the rush of polar air,
plates of ice, caught on the ebb,

saltings hanging from frozen rings
and, for a moment, the sea stops.

Loss

Two herons grace   this watercolour sky
trees are charcoal   rubbing mist

    over the land that shape-shifts

a pinnacle of song-thrush   stuck on fugue
then the geese   vocal veering   the same trajectory...

    poem in pieces   pouring with rain.

Sticky residue   from the balsam poplar
fills the air   with sweet violets

    to waft through eternity...

one beached whale   lying in the harbour
three thousand miles   from its cyclic route

    – dying is simple –

stop breathing   yet we cannot believe
willing the swill of sea   to take it back.

Morning flares into pink   sheep are inside themselves
horses looking over   to check where I'm heading

    the sea an end-stop to this

except   by the side of the road   a hewn off fox tail
pink-cord-fresh   flick of white   tossed here

    like everything wrong with the world.

I plant tulips, winter beans…

on a mild sun-patched afternoon,
look up to a sky aflame behind trees,

turn to the moon
caught like a seeded dandelion.

I remember this when I can't sleep.
You'd go downstairs, make tea,

sit with the clock, trying to
finish the crossword, rain lashing

the front window. Outside, no-one
stirring, no-one worrying about

incessant rain, unable to go back to bed.
I drift into doze, a sudden image

of you in a hooded raincoat,
worn out from no sleep…

*

you stand there telling me to hurry,
caught in the light, looking down

as if the sun lived underground
and mushroomed back overnight,

a pale moon-bud of itself;

a little red on your lips,
to try and mend these broken flowers,

your face in disbelief –
you never liked mess;

half hidden in the lay of your scarf,
something to lend a daughter –

a small oak chest, lined in velvet
opens on the buttons cut from our lives

slippery as rain.

Walking with Edward Thomas

Something about deeper into woods
sycamore leaves in star bursts

each kissing gate *the past hovering*

diagonal light to trodden ground
grass beaded in rain, robin vocals

pools to pick my way through
iron railings in low November halo

weather closing, continuous rain
dove-grey sweeping east, hold onto

this gateway...

*

freeze-dried leaves, wading through,
the woods in their bones

>   *and we did go and pick blackberries*
>   *and you did make jam –*

goldfinch flight-calls following
troupes of long-tailed tits,

>   *throwing sticks for chestnuts*
>   *kicking spiny cases –*

a robin's flitting song while I eat satsumas,
snapping dark chocolate so cold,

>   *filling satchels,*
>   *home to be simmered in an old pan –*

gathering dark with a rag-bag of words,
cobweb sun spinning gold threads on my eyelash.

I loved your crystal vase...

the council says we can leave your curtains
and the red carpet in the hall, on the stairs,

but the threadbare living room has to be
ripped up, back to Marley tiles, 1953;

> *so many vases...*

you and Dad buying one for me,
carrying it between you the mile walk home.

I care about your swathe of winter heather,
the red Camellia budding by the window...

*

> *thanking me at the end,*
> *like a foetal child in pain –*

I consider the Churchyard yew –
taking in rain, converting to blood,

a thousand years mounding the ground,
a tumulus to hold the souls –

> *how hard it is to die in your*
> *daughter's house –*

Sunday, sheltering underneath,
Thursday, its death-throe gaping wound,

throat exposed in an open scream
big enough for me to climb inside.

Little things…

pink jumper, grey pinafore,
white socks, new shoes

the door at the back,
mother seeing me to a desk – not many here yet,

turning round to where she was…

handing round straws
in the warm fug of classroom

coloured squares, scissors
and glue, Janet and John,

the teacher's
slap behind the knees that stings

because I can't say *yellow*

my mother made to stand and sing her reading in class
to overcome her stammer

takes my arm as she would have Dad's…

little things –
the African violet opening overnight

her overgrown iceberg roses
their powdered smell

fresh from daisy-chain days…
keeping my mother's silver thimble.

The sun's shrinking hole…

> *take this money*
> *to pay for our funerals*

Lily of the valley on your birthday,
heady bonnets in the kitchen

from your garden, my garden…
to measure your life in cups of tea,

out of Richmond station to visit Nan,
it's the Lyon's cafe –

red vinyl seats, steamed windows,
denting the end of a waxed straw in a glass of milk

while you wipe your nose with a handkerchief
and say *that's a nice cup of tea.*

Your daughter's painting on the dining room wall –
there's glory, or when I try to catch sunsets

from the front door – you had an eye for such things
if there hadn't been a war…

4.25 in the afternoon, shaggy heads
of our tea-stained hydrangeas

waiting for the last breath…

> not sure about words:
> *don't write any poems about me…*

The Right Kind of Snow

Under the cover of white surrender,
forcing settlement, cannot be ignored –
the kind of snow you want to roll in
over and over like the terrier outside…

> *occasionally I mind being childless,*
> *count forty-nine pips from a grapefruit*
> *the same morning I dream a child*

mothers and children out in the street,
sticky gloves, damp knees, trying to roll
a snowman in the puff of powder snow,
ten inches deep and falling…

> *how much richer it seems with 240 pennies*
> *in the pound – when it's all dozens*
> *and the twelve times table*

a father and daughter at the window
and I wave – a rush of snow dissolves
in my mouth – outstretched tongue –
laughing in the taste of effervescence…

> *then to hold a new born, such fingers,*
> *walking through these whispers*
> *and still it snows*

I never told you about her –
in the fine, sifting down, light as breath,
living at the end of my pen,

I call her Rose.

For the Love of Madonna Lilies, 1938

I exist, cyclonic, barometric
pressures, rising slowly,

with the blue sky of yesterday, when mother
is a girl in the garden with sisters and summer
white lilies are standing full bloom.

She is smiling.

Today I will plant madonna lilies,
for the love of a garden to smile in,
for the language of flowers,

when mother is a girl in the garden
with sisters and cool summer dresses,
white lilies in bloom and she is smiling.

www.ingramcontent.com/pod-product-compliance
Lightning Source LLC
LaVergne TN
LVHW041310080426
835510LV00009B/932